A Bible Journaling Challenge

29 November – 24 December 2015

Sara Laughed

For Kristen, who has walked beside me in good times and bad.
I look forward to many more journeys together.

CONTENTS

I

WELCOME

Welcome to *Advent Illustrated!* I am so excited to have you joining us as we go through the Bible together in preparation of Christmas. This challenge will be running from the first day of Advent, November 29th, to December 24th. Together, we will be going through select verses and stories of the Bible, from the creation narrative to the Nativity. This guide will walk you through the daily readings by giving you the verse and a creative prompt for each day of Advent. I'm so excited to get started!

2

ABOUT THIS CHALLENGE

"Bible journaling" is a creative and artistic way to connect with scripture. Some people write, paint, and stamp right in their Bibles, over the words or beside them. Others prefer the margins, or separate notebooks or printables. You may choose to illustrate verses, play around with lettering, scrapbook, or just take notes. Whatever you are comfortable with is fine.

Advent Illustrated is a Bible journaling challenge in which we as a community journal through the Advent season together. My goal is to give you the opportunity to connect with scripture in a new way, and as part of a group.

Every day of Advent (with the exception of Sundays), we will focus on a verse that fits into the story of the Bible. Sundays will be "grace days" to catch up or take a breather. Thursdays will be our "looking forward" days, where we step out of the Biblical story and look forward to the birth of Jesus. However much you want to participate is up to you! Whether you want to journal every day or just once a week, the schedules are set as guidelines, rather than rules. For more information on the plans we have available, check out Chapter 5.

How to use this guide

This guide is a collection of some of my more popular posts on Bible journaling to get you started if you are newer to the process. It then goes on to a few different options for plans that you can follow this Advent season, before digging in to the Biblical verses we will be illustrating, and providing some context and creative prompts for each. Reading the context and guidelines is *completely optional.* If you are struck by a verse and you have an idea that isn't in the guidelines, *go for it!* This challenge is all about creativity and connecting with the Bible in a new way. The prompts are here to facilitate that, but they are not mandatory in any way. Just have fun!

Fitting it all in

Some of the verses that I have chosen, especially those later on in the challenge as we walk through the New Testament, are quite close together. As a result, not every verse has its own page. There are a few ways that you can deal with this. I encourage you to take some time before you start the challenge to look at the verses we will be

9

working through, and maybe divide your pages accordingly. You could choose to illustrate half a page for one verse and the other half for the next, for example. You could also choose to do a neighboring page for some of the verses, if you prefer to have a lot of room. Finally, you can use our free Bible journaling page downloads to illustrate, if you don't have the space in your Bible, don't have a Bible, or would just prefer the extra room.

Where is the journaling community held?

The community will be held in a couple of places.

Facebook. I have created a closed Facebook group called "Advent Illustrated" that you are all encouraged to join! Similar to my favorite Bible journaling group, Journaling Bible Community, it is a place to share your work and gain encouragement. Any updates on the challenge, as well as daily prompt reminders and creative cues, will be shared there. This is where the meat of the challenge will be happening, so please read the community guidelines and join!

Instagram. My primary Instagram, full of seasonal photos and life updates, is over at SaraLaughed; but photos of my Bible journaling work are reserved for my second Instagram, SaraLaughedCreates. On that account, I will be uploading my own responses to the *Advent Illustrated* prompts, and will be tracking the hashtag #AdventIllustrated to see your beautiful work! My posts from the week, as well as my favorites of your posts, will be featured on that account AND on…

My blog! My blog, http://saralaughed.com, is my

"home base," where I will be sharing the full list of the season's verses and prompts, as well as a weekly round-up of my work and my favorites of your posts from Facebook and Instagram.

And now, a little word on community.

Participating. How much you want to participate in this challenge (or not) is totally up to you. You can journal with us every day and share it all online, or you can just observe and follow along. There is no requirement.

Sharing. This is supposed to be fun! Please don't worry about making something that isn't 'up to snuff.' If you made it and it was meaningful for you, then that's beautiful, and we want to see it! If you don't feel comfortable sharing with the whole wide world on Instagram, then you can share it in our private Facebook group, or you can just keep it to yourself.

Courtesy and kindness. It is extremely important to me that this challenge is welcoming, inviting, and accepting for anyone who wants to join. Whether you're new to Bible journaling or have been doing this for years; whether you're liberal or conservative, in politics or faith; whether you're from this denomination or that, or from no denomination at all; I want the *Advent Illustrated* community to be a place that is safe and welcoming for you. In order to maintain that kind of environment, we need the Facebook group and the comments on the blog posts to stay positive and encouraging. Posts that degrade, insult, or hurt each other are disrespectful and will not be accepted. Thank you for understanding!

With that in mind, let's get started with Bible journaling!

3

SUPPLIES

I'll start by saying that you need absolutely nothing to do Bible journaling other than a Bible and a pen. Really. You may have seen people with beautiful paints, stamps, and tabs in their Bibles, but all of those people got started with what you probably already have in your house.

That said, if you'd like to buy a special journaling Bible or you would like to invest in pens that don't bleed through thin paper, I have some recommendations.

Favorite Bible: Black ESV Single Column Journaling Bible by Crossway

Crossway has a very beautiful selection of Bibles that are specifically intended for Bible journaling. The one that I use, which is shown in the photo on the front page of this chapter, is the Black ESV single column journaling Bible. I love that it opens flat, whether you're flipping open to Genesis or Revelation. I also really love the cream-colored paper and the size and font of the text. For those of you who prefer a less plain option, Crossway also has a floral cloth over board Bible and an antique floral design.

Favorite pens: Sakura Pigma Micron 01 Ink Pen Set

Having used gel pens, rollerballs, and even my beloved Stabilo pens on Bible paper, I can say that bleed-through is a huge problem. It's frustrating, ugly, and it makes the other side of the paper harder to read. Pigma Micron pens are designed for archival paper, so the ink does not bleed through, even on very thin paper like that found in most Bibles. The tips are very fine, so it is easy to take small notes in the margins, or make bigger doodles.

Favorite highlighters: Zebra Eco Zebrite Double-Ended Highlighters

When it comes to liquid highlighters, these are my favorite for Bible journaling by far. They go on smoothly and don't bleed through the paper. I use the fine-tip highlighters so I can highlight line by line if I want to. As with the Pigma Micron pens, these highlighters "ghost" through the paper a little, meaning you can see a touch of color on the other side — but there is no bleed through, and the ghosting is less than I have had with any other product.

Other products

In addition to these products, I use colored pencils and watercolor pencils. Many other people use paints, stamps, and stickers — it's all up to you! Go through your house or your local craft store and find the things that inspire you. Good luck and have fun!

4

HOW TO START BIBLE JOURNALING

Many people participating in this challenge are excited to start Bible journaling, but don't know where to start. I know that taking notes in your Bible can be a little intimidating, let alone drawing, lettering, and painting in it! For that reason, this chapter will be a brief guide on how to get started in your journaling Bible for those of you who haven't yet. If you're already comfortable with Bible journaling, skip ahead to the next chapter to start the challenge!

Understanding what it's all about

Alright, let's get one thing clear: Bible journaling is not about making the most beautiful art. I, myself, am guilty of wanting to make something really beautiful and impressive for the sake of, well... making something really beautiful and impressive. But that's not the right attitude. Journaling isn't about the outcome, it's about the process. Focus on connecting with what you're doing, and the skill will come with time.

Finding a verse

You have your Bible, your pen(s), and maybe some extras, like paints, stamps, or stickers. The next thing to do is find a verse.

Bible journaling can be a little scary, especially if you're not used to writing in your Bible. I recommend starting off with a verse that you know well and that means a lot to you. Beginning with a verse that you are very familiar with helps take away some level of discomfort when it comes to journaling in your Bible for the first time, and it may spark an idea faster. But I stress choosing a verse you know and like before journaling your favorite verse. If you choose your absolute favorite, it may be difficult to come up with a design that includes everything it means to you. Start small until you're comfortable.

Getting inspired

I'm a creative soul, but I'm not an artistic soul. I

find it difficult to come up with entirely new designs for things. I like to find inspiration – and with the Internet, that's easier to do than ever. I use a Pinterest board.

You can also join a Bible journaling group on Facebook. My favorite is Shanna Noel's Journaling Bible Community. Or you can do a Google search for "Bible journaling" and the verse you chose, to see designs that other people have done with that same verse! Finding inspiration in places like these is a great way to get started with Bible journaling and figure out your style and the kinds of art you'd like to try.

Getting started

Alright, here comes the exciting part! Now that you have your tools and verse, it's time to get started. Everyone has a different process for how they do this; you may want to pray first, or jump right in. In the end, what it comes down to is mustering up the courage to put pen to paper and make something that expresses how you feel.

This is my method for the actual journaling process:

Reflect on the verse. Read it over a few times; maybe do a little background reading. Let it sink into your bones. I think about the parts of the verse that mean something to me, and then I try to figure out how I can represent them in art.

Sketch it out with a pencil. I like to use a simple mechanical pencil to do my sketching so that I don't make any permanent mistakes!

Outline it with pen. I use my skinny Pigma Microns to do this, as they don't bleed through the paper.

Fill it in with color. Next, I use gel pens, colored pencils, and watercolor pencils to add color and dimension to my design.

That's it! Everyone's process is different, but starting with simple colored pencils may be easier for those of you who haven't done Bible journaling before. Once you get more comfortable with Bible journaling, you can go ahead and experiment with paints, stamps, and stickers. The Word is your canvas!

5

SCHEDULE AND PLANS

I'm a planning girl. I like to make lists, schedules, and guidelines. As such, I've put together a few different options for how you can participate in this challenge. Each option comes at different levels of involvement, so you can choose a plan that fits your life and your schedule. What's most important is that you do what works for you. If you want to spend time every day getting creative in scripture, we've got you covered. If you can only carve out time once a week, there's an option for that too.

The program

Our Bible journaling challenge goes through the story of the Bible, starting with Genesis and ending with the Nativity. We will spend Mondays, Tuesdays, Wednesdays, Fridays, and Saturdays going through the story of the Bible as it is presented. Sundays are "grace days" that you can use to catch up or take a breather. Thursdays are our "looking forward" days, when we will step outside of the narrative of the Bible and look forward to the birth of Jesus.

Each day will come with a verse that our community will be journaling together. This guide will also include context and a creative prompt for each day, to give you some idea of where that day's verse fits into our Biblical story and to get your creative juices flowing. This chapter includes our calendar so you can see the whole month in review, and goes over each of the four "plans" that you can choose to follow. (Because I'm a little nerdy, I've named them after the first four fruits of the spirit!)

1. **Love** (6 days a week) Using this plan, you will participate in every day of our challenge, following along with the Biblical story *and* looking forward to the birth of Jesus by journaling with us on Thursdays.

2. **Joy** (5 days a week). This plan will have you following the Biblical story *only,* using both Thursdays and Sundays as "rest days". You can also modify it to have your weekends off by moving your Friday and Saturday verses forward by one day. The schedules for both of these plans are provided in the

pages ahead, so all the work has been done for you!

3. **Peace** (1 day a week). Here you will join us in looking forward to the birth of Jesus by journaling our Thursday verses only, at a pace of one journaling page per week.

4. **Patience** (only the last week). Advent is a busy time for many of us. If you don't have the time to prepare for Christmas all month long, you are welcome to join in at any time. However, you can also choose to join our Patience plan by journaling from Friday, November 18th to Thursday, December 24th. These days hold our New Testament verses, going from the announcement of Jesus' birth through the nativity story.

Calendar

There are also individualized schedules for each of the plans in the coming pages. A calendar of the month's daily verses is available on page 30.

LOVE – 6 DAYS A WEEK

Day	Date	Verse	Prompt
Sun	11/29	*Grace day*	*Grace day*
Mon	11/30	Genesis 1:1, John 1:1	Light
Tues	12/1	Genesis 1:31	Beauty
Wed	12/2	Genesis 3:6	Good and Evil
Thurs	12/3	Isaiah 7:14	Immanuel - God with us
Fri	12/4	Genesis 9:1	Rainbow
Sat	12/5	Genesis 22:17	Stars and sand
Sun	12/6	*Grace day*	*Grace day*
Mon	12/7	Genesis 28:12-16	House of God
Tues	12/8	Genesis 45:4-5, 8	Faith
Wed	12/9	Exodus 3:14-15	I am that I am
Thurs	12/10	Zechariah 9:9	King, donkey
Fri	12/11	Joshua 1:2-3	Fulfillment

Sat	12/12	Ruth 2:12	Refuge
Sun	12/13	*Grace day*	*Grace day*
Mon	12/14	1 Samuel 1:27-28	Giving to God
Tues	12/15	2 Samuel 6:14	Dancing for joy
Wed	12/16	Jonah 2:7	Prayer
Thurs	12/17	2 Corinthians 9:15	Gift
Fri	12/18	Luke 1:30-31	Promise
Sat	12/19	Luke 1:41	Joy
Sun	12/20	*Grace day*	*Grace day*
Mon	12/21	Luke 2:8-9	Shepherds
Tues	12/22	Matthew 2:10	Wise men
Wed	12/23	Luke 2:10-11	Baby Jesus
Thurs	12/24	Romans 15:13	Joy and peace

JOY – 5 DAYS A WEEK
GRACE DAYS ON THURS & SUN

Day	Date	Verse	Prompt
Sun	11/29	*Grace day*	*Grace day*
Mon	11/30	Genesis 1:1, John 1:1	Light
Tues	12/1	Genesis 1:31	Beauty
Wed	12/2	Genesis 3:6	Good and evil
Thurs	12/3	*Grace day*	*Grace day*
Fri	12/4	Genesis 9:1	Rainbow
Sat	12/5	Genesis 22:17	Stars and sand
Sun	12/6	*Grace day*	*Grace day*
Mon	12/7	Genesis 28:12-16	House of God
Tues	12/8	Genesis 45:4-5, 8	Faith
Wed	12/9	Exodus 3:14-15	I am that I am
Thurs	12/10	*Grace day*	*Grace day*
Fri	12/11	Joshua 1:2-3	Fulfillment
Sat	12/12	Ruth 2:12	Refuge

Sun	12/13	*Grace day*	*Grace day*
Mon	12/14	1 Samuel 1:27-28	Giving to God
Tues	12/15	2 Samuel 6:14	Dancing for joy
Wed	12/16	Jonah 2:7	Prayer
Thurs	12/17	*Grace day*	*Grace day*
Fri	12/18	Luke 1:30-31	Promise
Sat	12/19	Luke 1:41	Joy
Sun	12/20	*Grace day*	*Grace day*
Mon	12/21	Luke 2:8-9	Shepherds
Tues	12/22	Matthew 2:10	Wise men
Wed	12/23	Luke 2:10-11	Baby Jesus
Thurs	12/24	*Grace day*	*Grace day*

JOY – 5 DAYS A WEEK
GRACE DAYS ON WEEKENDS

Day	Date	Verse	Prompt
Sun	11/29	*Grace day*	*Grace day*
Mon	11/30	Genesis 1:1, John 1:1	Light
Tues	12/1	Genesis 1:31	Beauty
Wed	12/2	Genesis 3:6	Good and Evil
Thurs	12/3	Genesis 9:1	Rainbow
Fri	12/4	Genesis 22:17	Stars and sand
Sat	12/5	*Grace day*	*Grace day*
Sun	12/6	*Grace day*	*Grace day*
Mon	12/7	Genesis 28:12-16	House of God
Tues	12/8	Genesis 45:4-5, 8	Faith
Wed	12/9	Exodus 3:14-15	I am that I am
Thurs	12/10	Joshua 1:2-3	Fulfillment
Fri	12/11	Ruth 2:12	Refuge
Sat	12/12	*Grace day*	*Grace day*

Sun	12/13	*Grace day*	*Grace day*
Mon	12/14	1 Samuel 1:27-28	Giving to God
Tues	12/15	2 Samuel 6:14	Dancing for joy
Wed	12/16	Jonah 2:7	Prayer
Thurs	12/17	Luke 1:30-31	Promise
Fri	12/18	Luke 1:41	Joy
Sat	12/19	*Grace day*	*Grace day*
Sun	12/20	*Grace day*	*Grace day*
Mon	12/21	Luke 2:8-9	Shepherds
Tues	12/22	Matthew 2:10	Wise men
Wed	12/23	Luke 2:10-11	Baby Jesus
Thurs	12/24	*Grace day*	*Grace day*

PEACE – 1 DAY A WEEK

Day	Date	Verse	Prompt
Thurs	12/3	Isaiah 7:14	Immanuel - God with us
Thurs	12/10	Zechariah 9:9	King, donkey
Thurs	12/17	2 Corinthians 9:15	Gift
Thurs	12/24	Romans 15:13	Joy and peace

Those on the Love plan will be completing these entries on Thursdays, but please don't feel that you *need* to do your journaling on Thursdays, too. Just do it on the day that feels right for you, and share with the group when you like.

PATIENCE – LAST WEEK
OF ADVENT

Day	Date	Verse	Prompt
Fri	12/18	Luke 1:30-31	Promise
Sat	12/19	Luke 1:41	Joy
Sun	12/20	*Grace day*	*Grace day*
Mon	12/21	Luke 2:8-9	Shepherds
Tues	12/22	Matthew 2:10	Wise men
Wed	12/23	Luke 2:10-11	Baby Jesus
Thurs	12/24	Romans 15:13	Joy and peace

Sunday *Grace Day*	Monday *Biblical story*	Tuesday *Biblical story*	Wednesday *Biblical story*	Thursday *Looking forward*	Friday *Biblical story*	Saturday *Biblical story*
29 *Grace Day*	**30** Gen 1:1 Light	**1** Gen 1:31 Beauty	**2** Gen 3:6 Good and Evil	**3** *Isaiah 7:14* Immanuel	**4** Gen 9:1 Rainbow	**5** Gen 22:17 Stars and sand
6 *Grace Day*	**7** Gen 28:12-16 House of God	**8** Gen 45:4-5,8 Faith, forgiveness	**9** Ex 3:14-15 I am that I am	**10** *Zechariah 9:9* King, donkey	**11** Joshua 1:2-3 Fulfillment	**12** Ruth 2:12 Refuge
13 *Grace Day*	**14** 1 Sam 1:27-28 Giving to God	**15** 2 Sam 6:14 Dancing for joy	**16** Jonah 2:7 Prayer	**17** *2 Corinthians 9:15* Gift	**18** Luke 1:30-31 Promise	**19** Luke 1:41 Joy
20 *Grace Day*	**21** Luke 2:8-9 Shepherds	**22** Matthew 2:10 Wise men	**23** *Luke 2:10-11* Baby Jesus	**24** *Romans 15:13* Joy and peace		

6

ADVENT SELECTIONS

Hooray! It's time to dig into your Bible. These verses have been chosen as excerpts of different stages in the Biblical story, from the creation accounts to the Nativity. This guide includes the verses, which are taken from the ESV, and creative prompts for those of us who struggle with ideas — however, each member is encouraged to interpret and illustrate the verse in their own way. Our differences are what make us beautiful!

SUNDAY, NOVEMBER 29

—

GRACE DAY

I am sure that you are just as excited as I am to get started on this creative journey through scripture together. Today is a day to prepare yourself for the month ahead, physically and spiritually. If you have not yet set up a space in which to do your Bible journaling, or if you don't yet have all your supplies, today is the day to take that step.

Spiritually, this is a time to make some room in your heart for the weeks ahead. Advent is a beautiful time of preparation, but it can also be stressful and overwhelming as we prepare for the hustle and bustle of Christmas day. Make sure that you are doing your best to take care of yourself during this busy time, and be ready to set aside some time for Bible journaling on whatever basis your life permits.

We are so happy to have you joining us, and welcome to the Advent season!

—
GENESIS 1:1, JOHN 1:1

Verse:

*In the beginning, God created the heavens and the earth. The earth
was without form and void, and darkness was over the face of the
deep. And the Spirit of God was hovering over the face of the waters.
And God said, "Let there be light," and there was light. And God
saw that the light was good.*

Genesis 1:1-4

*In the beginning was the Word, and the Word was with
God, and the Word was God. He was in the beginning with God.
All things were made through him, and without him was not any
thing made that was made. In him was life, and the life was the light
of men. The light shines in the darkness, and the darkness has not
overcome it.*

John 1:1-5

Context and prompt:

Here we have two verses that tell us a story: the
beginning, as the Bible tells it. Consider how these two
verses describe light. Genesis says that it was the first thing
to be created, and John tells us that the life found in Jesus
is "the light of men," which "shines in the darkness" and
has not been overcome.

Using these verses, illustrate *light* on your page. You

could use watercolor paints or pencils to 'shine light' on the page, or draw a sun, or even a light bulb! If you prefer words to pictures, try lettering the phrase "Let there be light," or the lyrics to a light-related song ("I'm walking on sunshine..."). Play with the idea of the birth of light and *have fun*! There's no wrong way to do this. Just break out your tools and get started.

TUESDAY, DECEMBER 1
—
GENESIS 1:31

Verse:

And God saw everything that he had made, and behold, it was very good.

Genesis 1:31

Context and prompt:

This verse takes place after God has created the world. He takes a step back to see everything He had made, and He sees it is good. Today, we are doing the same, by reflecting on the beauty of the world and the richness of life. You could use your supplies to sketch out the Garden of Eden, filled with the "beasts of the earth and the birds of the heavens" that we learn about in Genesis 1. You could draw the beauty you see outside your bedroom window, or something breathtaking you see in the world. Celebrate the beauty of the world today in the pages of your Bible!

WEDNESDAY, DECEMBER 2
—
GENESIS 3:6

Verse:

So when the woman saw that the tree was good for food, and that it was a delight to the eyes, and that the tree was to be desired to make one wise, she took of its fruit and ate, and she also gave some to her husband who was with her, and he ate.

Genesis 3:6

Context and prompt:

Most of us know the story of Adam and Eve. Many of us have heard this tale since we were children. For some, it is uncomfortable; but it is an important story when we look at the arc of the Bible. It sets up the rest of Genesis and the Old Testament. And while Genesis and the Gospels were written many miles and years apart, by different people in different languages, this story also prepares us for the birth of Jesus!

Today's prompt is to reflect the tree of knowledge of good and evil. Each of us carries the potential for good and evil within us; each of us lives with triumph and with struggle. You may imagine the tree holding those good and bad things — your strengths and weaknesses. Or you may imagine it as just looking like an apple tree, with healthy and rotten apples. However it looks to you, let that imagery guide you in journaling in your Bible today.

THURSDAY, DECEMBER 3
—
ISAIAH 7:14

Verse:

Therefore the Lord himself will give you a sign. Behold, the virgin shall conceive and bear a son, and shall call his name Immanuel.
Isaiah 7:14

Context and prompt:

This is our 'looking forward' day, in which we step out of the Biblical story to look forward to the birth of Jesus. Today we read a verse from Isaiah, which looks forward to the birth of the Messiah and says that his name shall be Immanuel. We know from Matthew 1:23 that the name Immanuel means "God with us."

Today, use your excitement and anticipation for Christmas day to illustrate this verse. You could draw a picture of Mary in her pregnancy, or of the baby Jesus in a manger. Or you could think about the meaning of Immanuel, and what it means for God to be with us in spirit or in flesh. Whatever direction you go in, have fun with this verse and let it inspire you to be creative in the pages of your Bible.

FRIDAY, DECEMBER 4

—

GENESIS 9:13-17

Verse:

"I have set my bow in the cloud, and it shall be a sign of the covenant between me and the earth. When I bring clouds over the earth and the bow is seen in the clouds, I will remember my covenant that is between me and you and every living creature of all flesh. And the waters shall never again become a flood to destroy all flesh. When the bow is in the clouds, I will see it and remember the everlasting covenant between God and every living creature of all flesh that is on the earth." God said to Noah, "This is the sign of the covenant that I have established between me and all flesh that is on the earth."

Genesis 9:13-17

Context and prompt:

The story of Noah's ark is almost as famous as that of Adam and Eve. When we think of it, we think of the animals going into the ark, side by side. We think of the flood waters rising, of the days and nights spent inside the ark, and of the dove finally finding an olive leaf that meant safe ground. But we don't as often think of the covenant that God makes with Noah. It echoes the covenants that come before and after it; the promises that God makes to His people. To symbolize that covenant, God creates the rainbow.

Today, consider the rainbow as the symbol of

God's promise. Think of the rich colors and how it symbolizes the peace and sunshine after a storm. Take out your colored pencils, your paints, or your stamps, and have fun!

SATURDAY, DECEMBER 5

– GENESIS 22:17

Verse:

"I will surely bless you, and I will surely multiply your offspring as the stars of heaven and as the sand that is on the seashore."

Genesis 22:17

Context and prompt:

The stars of heaven and the sand on the seashore - what beautiful imagery! This verse comes after a very challenging moment in the story of Abraham, but the trial is followed by another one of God's promises. God promises Abraham that he will be the father of a great nation, which will number as many as the stars in the sky or the sand on the shore.

Let the imagery inspire you. You could sketch the sky along the top of the page, and the ocean along the bottom. Because the stars and sand represent the descendants of Abraham, you could also draw the 'stars' in your own family line, writing the names of your family members as stars in the sky on your page. Just enjoy the imagery and find a way to connect with it on your page today.

SUNDAY, DECEMBER 6
—
GRACE DAY

In just six days we walked from the birth of light to the promises made to Abraham. On Thursday we looked forward to Christmas day by thinking of the meaning of Immanuel — God with us.

Today is our "grace day." Use this day to rest and relax, or to catch up on a verse that you may have missed or skipped throughout the week. Whatever you do, try to take some time for you today during this busy season!

You may also want to take this time to upload a few photos of your work from this week, either to the Facebook group (Advent Illustrated) or to Instagram with the hashtag #AdventIllustrated. This is a great way for us to see each other's work and be inspired by one another.

GENESIS 28:12-16

Verse:

And he dreamed, and behold, there was a ladder set up on the earth, and the top of it reached to heaven. And behold, the angels of God were ascending and descending on it! And behold, the Lord stood above it and said, "I am the Lord, the God of Abraham your father and the God of Isaac... Behold, I am with you and will keep you wherever you go, and will bring you back to this land. For I will not leave you until I have done what I have promised you." Then Jacob awoke from his sleep and said, "Surely the Lord is in this place, and I did not know it."

Genesis 28:12-16

Context and prompt:

This story takes place when Jacob, the grandson of Abraham, is running from his brother Esau. He finds a place to sleep and dreams of a ladder that goes from the earth into the heavens. There's a lot going on in this piece of text. We have the ladder, connecting the earth to the sky; we have God's promise to Jacob that He will not leave Jacob until He has done what He has promised; and we have Jacob's revelation that God is in this place, though he did not know it. When Jacob wakes up, he names the place Bethel, meaning *house of God*.

Reflect on these words today. How might God be

in *this place* — with you, around you — while you might not know it? Use your supplies to illustrate what this means to you. Get creative and have fun!

TUESDAY, DECEMBER 8
–
GENESIS 45:4-5, 8

Verse:

*So Joseph said to his brothers, "Come near to me, please."
And they came near. And he said, "I am your brother, Joseph, whom
you sold into Egypt. And now do not be distressed or angry with
yourselves because you sold me here, for God sent me before you to
preserve life... So it was not you who sent me here, but God."*
Genesis 45:4-5, 8

Context and prompt:

From Jacob, we move on to Joseph, Jacob's son. Joseph is Jacob's most beloved child, and Joseph's brothers sell him into slavery out of jealousy. Ultimately, Joseph rises to a position of power in Egypt, and has the strength of character to forgive his brothers for what they did to him.

Consider the themes of *forgiveness* and *faith*. Joseph is able to forgive his brothers for what they have done to him, despite the difficulty of his life after his brothers sold him into slavery. He also says that *God* sent him to Egypt, rather than his brothers. What does this attitude say about Joseph and his faith? How might this inspire you?

Play around with these ideas. Today's verse is a little abstract, so instead of illustrating the scene, consider illustrating what forgiveness or faith means to you.

WEDNESDAY, DECEMBER 9
—
EXODUS 3:14-15

Verse:

God said to Moses, "I am who I am." And he said, "Say this to the people of Israel, 'I am has sent me to you.'" God also said to Moses, "Say this to the people of Israel, 'The Lord, the God of your fathers, the God of Abraham, the God of Isaac, and the God of Jacob, has sent me to you.' This is my name forever, and thus I am to be remembered throughout all generations."

Exodus 3:14-15

Context and prompt:

This verse comes immediately after Moses first sees God in the burning bush. He takes off his shoes because he is standing on holy ground. When God tells Moses to go to Egypt to demand the freedom of the Hebrew people, Moses asks whom he should say sent him, and God responds with the words above. He calls Himself "The God of your fathers, the God of Abraham, the God of Isaac, the God of Jacob," and utters the famous words "I am who I am."

Today we reflect on the burning bush. You may want to illustrate the scene, drawing Moses before the bush, or the bush engulfed in a fire that doesn't burn it. If you are inspired by the line about the God of Abraham, Isaac, and Jacob, you could consider representing it with symbols — Abraham is traditionally represented by stars or a tent, Isaac by a ram, and Jacob by a ladder. Or you may want to play with the language "I am who I am," thinking about the identity of God and who God is to you. Use your imagination and let the richness of this text inspire you.

THURSDAY, DECEMBER 10
—
ZECHARIAH 9:9

Verse:

"Rejoice greatly, O daughter of Zion!
Shout, O daughter of Jerusalem!
Behold, your King is coming to you;
He is just and having salvation,
Lowly and riding on a donkey,
A colt, the foal of a donkey.

Zechariah 9:9

Context and prompt:

This is our 'looking forward' day, in which we step out of the Biblical story to look forward to the birth of Jesus. Today we look at a verse from Zechariah, which tells us about the coming of the King to the world. We know that He is coming to us - and in just a few short weeks, He will be, in the form of the baby Jesus on Christmas day!

As we prepare for that day, use this verse to connect with the pages of your Bible. You may want to draw Jesus on a donkey, such as during his triumphant entry on a donkey in John 12:14 (a story that we usually read around Easter time). You many want to draw Jesus as King, as the verse says. There are no rules; just focus on the imagery of this passage and how it feels to you, and try to express that today on the page before you.

FRIDAY, DECEMBER 11
–
JOSHUA 1:2-3

Verse:

"Now therefore arise, go over this Jordan, you and all this people, into the land that I am giving to them, to the people of Israel. Every place that the sole of your foot will tread upon I have given to you, just as I promised to Moses."

Joshua 1:2-3

Context and prompt:

After 40 years of leading the Israelites, Moses has died before he was able to enter the Promised Land. Joshua, however, is ready to lead the people into Canaan, the land flowing with milk and honey. Here, God tells him to cross over the Jordan and enter the land that He had promised to Moses. This verse is the beginning of the fulfillment of that promise.

You may choose to illustrate the land of milk and honey, where the soles of the feet of the Israelites will tread, as God had promised. Or you may choose to draw just that - a foot treading on promised ground. Today's verse is about the fulfillment of promises, so you may also want to look at how you experience that fulfillment in your own life. As I've said before, there is no way to go wrong — just let the verse speak to you, and do your best to connect with it on the page today.

SATURDAY, DECEMBER 12
—
RUTH 2:12

Verse:

"The Lord repay you for what you have done, and a full reward be given you by the Lord, the God of Israel, under whose wings you have come to take refuge!"

Ruth 2:12

Context and prompt:

Ruth is one of my favorite books of the Bible. During the time of the judges, which we know as a dark time full of corruption and moral decay, we meet Ruth. Ruth is a young Moabite woman who stays with her mother-in-law Naomi, even after Ruth's husband — the man connecting them — has died. Ruth chooses to follow Naomi's God (the Hebrew God) and come with her to Israel, where Naomi is from.

In this verse, Boaz, the family's future kinsman-redeemer, tells Ruth that she will be rewarded for her faithfulness to Naomi. I love the imagery here, of Ruth taking refuge under the wings of God. You may want to illustrate these words quite literally, with an eagle or dove stretching out its protective wings. Or you may choose to draw the words that Boaz speaks to Ruth in a way that is meaningful to you. Play with this verse and think about the themes of refuge and faithfulness and how you can express them today.

SUNDAY, DECEMBER 13
—
GRACE DAY

Today is our grace day, where we take some time to bounce back from the week and prepare for the coming days. Take some time for yourself today, or use it as an opportunity to catch up on a verse you may have missed during the week!

You may also want to use this time to take some photos of your work this week and share them with the community. You can do this in the Facebook group (Advent Illustrated) or on Instagram using the hashtag #AdventIllustrated. I am excited to see your work!

MONDAY, DECEMBER 14

—

I SAMUEL 1:27-28

Verse:

"For this child I prayed, and the Lord has granted me my petition that I made to him. Therefore I have lent him to the Lord. As long as he lives, he is lent to the Lord."
And he worshiped the Lord there.

1 Samuel 1:27-28

Context and prompt:

Hannah wanted a baby, but God had closed her womb. We know that Hannah was so distraught that she cried constantly and could not eat. Finally, she turned to prayer and she poured out her soul before God (1 Samuel 1:15), promising God that if He gave her a child, she would give the child back to Him and make her child a faithful servant of God. God remembered her and gave her a son.

As with many of the verses we have chosen, you can take this verse in a few different directions. You could illustrate Hannah praying in 1 Samuel 1, asking for her baby. You could draw the baby, Samuel, whose life was given to God. Or you could play with the words of "lending him to the Lord" and think of what it means to live a life that has been given to God, and what that means to you. Whatever direction you choose, have fun with it!

TUESDAY, DECEMBER 15
—
2 SAMUEL 6:14

Verse:

And David danced before the Lord with all his might.

2 Samuel 6:14

Context and prompt:

David had a heart for God. He loved God and feared God, rejoiced in God, wrote beautiful poetry for God, and danced before God "with all his might." In this verse, David brings the ark of God to the city of David and rejoices there, with dancing and celebration. We know that his wife Michal saw David dancing and despised him, later mocking him for embarrassing himself in front of the servants. David responds by saying, "I will make myself yet more contemptible than this" (2 Samuel 6:22), meaning that he is not afraid to embarrass himself in worshipping God, no matter what others think.

Use these verses to guide you today. You can think about David dancing, or draw a dancer using her art to celebrate the glory of God. You could also think about David's words in 2 Samuel 6:22. David worshipped God without fearing for embarrassment or judgment from others. What does that mean to you? Whichever direction you take this verse in, have fun with them in the pages of your Bible today.

WEDNESDAY, DECEMBER 16
—
JONAH 2:7

Verse:

*"When my life was fainting away,
I remembered the Lord,
and my prayer came to you,
into your holy temple."*

Jonah 2:7

Context and prompt:

Many of us are familiar with the story of Jonah. God asks Jonah to preach at Nineveh, and Jonah is afraid of the task and runs away. God responds by having a great fish (or whale, as we often tell it) swallow Jonah. In the belly of the fish, Jonah lets out a beautiful prayer, God releases him, and Jonah preaches at Nineveh as God had asked of him.

Today we look at this verse, in which Jonah talks about his life "fainting away" and remembering God during that difficult time. We have all had struggles and hard times in our lives, and often those are the times when we turn to God. You can play around with that idea, and think of what it means to you to turn to God when your life is fainting away *and* when it is holding strong. Or you can think of Jonah and the fish, drawing them as you see them in your mind. Dig into this verse and enjoy!

THURSDAY, DECEMBER 17
—
2 CORINTHIANS 9:15

Verse:

Thanks be to God for his inexpressible gift!
Corinthians 9:15

Context and prompt:

This is our 'looking forward' day, in which we step out of the Biblical story to look forward to the birth of Christ. Today we look at a verse from Corinthians, in which Paul is expressing gratitude for the inexpressible gift of Jesus.

Christmas is a time of gift giving, and we often associate the holiday with presents under the tree. If you like, you can use that imagery to guide you today as you think of the gift of the baby Jesus. You can also take it in a different direction, thinking about what inexpressible gifts God has give you throughout your life. This is a verse of celebration and awe; use that spirit of excitement and gratitude to guide you as you play around with this verse.

FRIDAY, DECEMBER 18
—
LUKE 1:30-31

Verse:

And the angel said to her, "Do not be afraid, Mary, for you have found favor with God. And behold, you will conceive in your womb and bear a son, and you shall call his name Jesus."
Luke 1:30-31

Context and prompt:

This famous scene, which has been illustrated time and time again in paintings and other artwork, sticks with us for a reason. Mary is a young girl, likely afraid and overwhelmed by the news that the angel Gabriel gives her. We don't know how she responds, but we know the angel's words are inspiring and comforting. *Do not be afraid. You have found favor with God.*

As we prepare for Christmas day, let these verses into your heart and imagine how Mary must have felt. You could illustrate her and the angel, taking a cue from some of the famous artists who have come before you. Or you could go in your own direction, playing around with the words that stand out in this verse. Don't be afraid to get creative and play around with the ideas that come to you. Let some of your excitement and anticipation for Christmas day guide you as you journal this page.

SATURDAY, DECEMBER 19

—

LUKE 1:41

Verse:

And when Elizabeth heard the greeting of Mary, the baby leaped in her womb. And Elizabeth was filled with the Holy Spirit.
Luke 1:41

Context and prompt:

Mary goes to Elizabeth, a family member and mentor. Elizabeth, too, is pregnant — pregnant with John the Baptist, who leaps in her womb when Mary greets Elizabeth.

There are many ways to go with this verse. You may choose to illustrate Mary and Elizabeth together, or draw John leaping for joy in his mother's womb. You can sketch out the scene, or express the feelings and emotions that you experience when reading these lines. Think of the excitement and joy in this passage and how it relates to your own feelings about the Christmas season. Let those feelings guide you as you get creative in the pages of your Bible today.

SUNDAY, DECEMBER 20

—

GRACE DAY

With Christmas only a few days away, take this time to rest and prepare yourself for the last few days of Advent. Today is your "grace day," so catch up on what you've missed or spend some time focusing on yourself during the hustle and bustle of the holiday season!

At this time, you may also wish to share some photos of your week's illustrations with the community. You can upload them to the Facebook group (Advent Illustrated), or to Instagram using the hashtag #AdventIllustrated. I look forward to seeing your artwork!

MONDAY, DECEMBER 21
–
LUKE 2:8-10

Verse:

And in the same region there were shepherds out in the field, keeping watch over their flock by night. And an angel of the Lord appeared to them, and the glory of the Lord shone around them, and they were filled with great fear. And the angel said to them, "Fear not, for behold, I bring you good news of great joy that will be for all the people."

Luke 2:8-10

Context and prompt:

As we get closer to the birth of Jesus, we meet the shepherds. An angel of God comes to them and tells them "good news of great joy that will be for all the people." That news is of the birth of Jesus!

Think of what *good news* and *great joy* means to you. You may want to illustrate this scene, with the angel hovering above the shepherds as they are out in the field by night. You may want to take this verse in a more abstract direction, focusing again on the anticipation and joy that lingers in this passage. Get excited as we approach Christmas day along with the shepherds, and let that excitement guide you in your journaling entry.

TUESDAY, DECEMBER 22
—
MATTHEW 2:10

Verse:

When they saw the star, they rejoiced exceedingly with great joy.

Matthew 2:10

Context and prompt:

Now we meet the three wise men, who see the star and know that it will help them find Jesus. Like the last verse and the one before it, this is a joyful verse, full of excitement and anticipation and joy. You may or may not be feeling many of these same things as we approach Christmas day.

For today's verse, you may choose to draw the three wise men, traveling with their gifts. Or you may decide to draw the star which shines above the place of Jesus' birth, though the wise men likely arrived after Jesus was born. Tomorrow we will be illustrating the baby Jesus, so use this day to get out your feelings of joy and preparation as we travel with the wise men. Take it in whatever direction you want!

WEDNESDAY, DECEMBER 23
–
LUKE 2:11-12

Verse:

For unto you is born this day in the city of David a Savior, who is Christ the Lord. And this will be a sign for you: you will find a baby wrapped in swaddling cloths and lying in a manger."
Luke 2:11-12

Context and prompt:

Today, two days before Christmas, we think of the baby who is born in a manger in the city of David. We think of the peace and love that this small baby brings us. You may choose to illustrate the baby Jesus today, or to play with the words in this verse and illustrate those that speak to you. Experience the joy of these lines as we celebrate the birth of the Prince of Peace, the King of Kings, "Christ the Lord!" Celebrate the birth in the pages of your Bible today!

THURSDAY, DECEMBER 24
—
ROMANS 15:13

Verse:

May the God of hope fill you with all joy and peace in believing, so that by the power of the Holy Spirit you may abound in hope.

Romans 15:13

Context and prompt:

Today is our final day of Advent, and the last day that we will be Bible journaling together. Yesterday we illustrated the verses that welcomed Jesus into the world. Today, the last day before Christmas, we reflect on what the life and teachings of Jesus bring us: joy and hope.

On this last day of Advent and of our challenge, there are no guidelines. Let this verse speak to you and illustrate it in whatever way feels right. Dig in, have fun, and celebrate!

CLOSING WORDS

Wow, what a month! Thank you so much for joining us this Advent season. I hope that this challenge was a fun and rewarding experience for you.

I also hope that, no matter what plan you were using or how often you journaled, at the end of this journey you have given yourself a gift. Perhaps it is a deeper or different appreciation of the Bible than you had when you came in. Perhaps it is your Bible, now filled with your artwork, which you can continue to use in the coming years. Perhaps it is an heirloom Bible that you can pass onwards, full of illustrations and artwork that will be cherished for generations to come. Whatever you have gained, I pray it stays with you long after this holiday season.

Thank you for joining us in this challenge, and Merry Christmas!

ABOUT THE AUTHOR

Sara Laughed is a writer, blogger, and student of religion. She writes about life, love, faith, and wellness at her blog, http://saralaughed.com.

Made in the USA
Lexington, KY
14 December 2015